Love, Jesus

Letters of Divine Hope for Tinnitus Sufferers

Lisa Bristow

Seishi Press

Copyright

Preface

Dear beloved tinnitus warrior,

I was not planning to write this book at all. These letters of hope came to me during quiet times with Jesus, and I had absolutely no plan to show them to anyone else. But God had other ideas. And, after much prayer, and with some nervousness, here they are!

This is a book of hope for anyone who needs comfort in their struggles with tinnitus. It reminds us that, even when it feels like Jesus is distant, he is much closer than we realise. In fact, he's walking right beside us on every step of our tinnitus journey.

If you're struggling with a particular situation, you can take a look at the contents pages to find a letter written for just that challenge. Or you may want to leaf through the book until you find a letter of hope or some words of scripture that lighten your heart.

Whichever letter or quote you choose, I invite you to pause, take some moments to ponder what you read, and allow the words of comfort and reassurance to soak into your heart and mind.

I pray this book offers comfort and inspiration to all tinnitus warriors. Remember, beloved one, that Jesus cares for each and every one of us, with a never-ending love.

Love,

Lisa

Contents

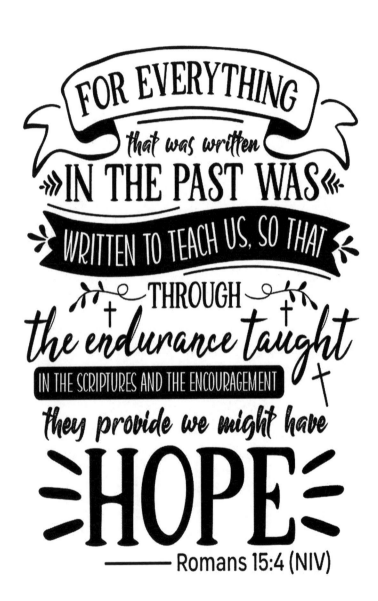

FOR EVERYTHING *that was written* IN THE PAST WAS WRITTEN TO TEACH US, SO THAT THROUGH *the endurance taught* IN THE SCRIPTURES AND THE ENCOURAGEMENT *they provide we might have* HOPE

— Romans 15:4 (NIV)

When you get your diagnosis

Dear beloved tinnitus warrior,

I see you. I see you sitting in your car after your ENT appointment, gasping in disbelief that you've been told, "You've just got to learn to live with your tinnitus".

I see how hard you're trying to blink back tears of shock and bewilderment that there is no cure, and the doctors can't help you. And I know that your tinnitus is shouting because of the distress and the anger and the feeling of being abandoned to cope with this extraordinary noise on your own.

But hear this. You are **not** alone. I understand what it's like to have tinnitus. And I'm here to walk alongside you on every step of your tinnitus journey.

I've got you. And together we've got this.

Love,

Jesus

"FOR I KNOW THE

plans

I Have For You,"

DECLARES THE LORD,

"PLANS TO

prosper you

AND NOT TO HARM YOU,

PLANS
TO GIVE YOU

hope

AND A FUTURE" Jeremiah
29:11 (NIV)

When you feel angry

Dear beloved tinnitus warrior,

I see you. I see how frustrated and angry you are at the injustice of getting tinnitus. Maybe you're the only one of your friends to get tinnitus after years of loud gigs. Maybe your employer should have given you hearing protection. Maybe the tinnitus has appeared with no obvious cause.

I have broad shoulders, so bring your anger to me. I can take it; in fact I welcome it. I offer you a sanctuary, a safe space where you can let all those feelings out without hurting your friends or family.

Bring it all. Come and shout at me, and shake your fist at me. Tell me how bad things feel at the moment, and how unfair life is. Keep going until you get everything out of your system. I can absorb all your fury and your frustration. It won't hurt me, though it makes me sad to see you – a beloved child of our Father – suffering so deeply.

And when you have finished, I will hold you. When you have nothing left to say and tears come in place of words, I will comfort you. I will restore you.

Love,

Jesus

Blessed

ARE THOSE WHO TRUST IN

THE LORD

AND HAVE MADE

The Lord

THEIR HOPE AND

CONFIDENCE

JEREMIAH 17:7 (NLT)

When you blame yourself

Dear beloved tinnitus warrior,

I see you. I see that you're ashamed and blaming yourself for causing your tinnitus.

Listen to me! It's not your fault. You didn't ask for tinnitus, so don't blame yourself.

It doesn't matter to me whether you spent years standing in front of the speaker at concerts or maxing out the volume of your head-phones.

All of that is in the past, and I am all about the life to come. I'm focused on what could be, rather than what has been and gone.

So tell me, beloved child of God, what will you do today to create your wonder-filled future?

Love,

Jesus

LET YOUR UNFAILING
love
»» SURROUND US ««
LORD FOR OUR
HOPE
IS IN YOU ALONE
•Psalm 33:22 (NLT)•

When you lie awake at 3am

Dear beloved tinnitus warrior,

I see you. I see you awake at 3am, tossing and turning in your bed. All you can hear in the quiet of the night is your tinnitus, and the sound is overwhelming.

I know how it is to be the only one awake – in your house, in your neighbourhood. How lonely you feel when everyone else in the world seems to be sleeping peacefully.

I see those anxious thoughts running through your head. What happens if I can't get back to sleep? How will I function tomorrow? Will I ever be able to sleep through the night again?

And I want you to know that you **will** get through tonight, and any other disturbed night that tinnitus may bring. And you know what? You can function on a lot less sleep than you think.

I understand what it's like to be you right now. I'm here, holding you in your pain and your hurt. I've got you. You are not alone. You are my beloved.

Love,

Jesus

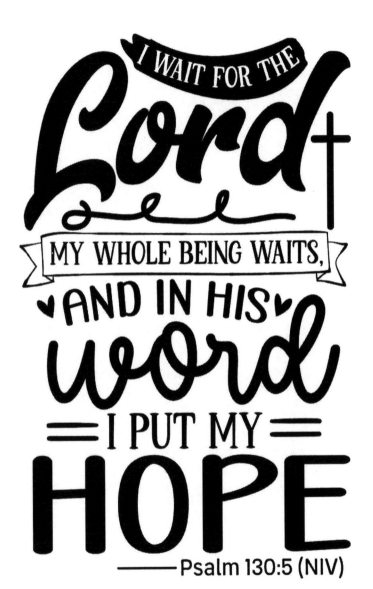

I WAIT FOR THE Lord† MY WHOLE BEING WAITS, AND IN HIS word I PUT MY HOPE

—Psalm 130:5 (NIV)

When you feel exhausted

Dear beloved tinnitus warrior,

I see you. I see you're so tired, you're struggling to put one foot in front of the other.

Tinnitus is exhausting, I know that. And I want you to remember that I understand what you're going through, even if others in your life don't get it.

Come to me and rest. Press pause on the things of this world, and step into mine. You don't need to pray or worship. You don't need to say anything - I already know how difficult this is for you.

Let's just rest together, side by side, and breathe; each of us enjoying the other's presence. You can lean on me for as long as you like until you feel strong enough to get going again.

I'll always be here for you, whenever you need to pause.

Love,

Jesus

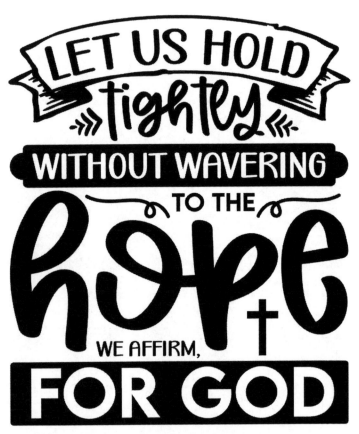

LET US HOLD *tightey* WITHOUT WAVERING TO THE *hope* WE AFFIRM, FOR GOD CAN BE TRUSTED TO KEEP *his promise*

Hebrews 10:23 (NLT)

When you struggle with a spike

Dear beloved tinnitus warrior,

I see you. I can feel all your fear and anxiety and distress as you listen to this tinnitus spike.

I see you looking back over the past few days, desperate to find something that might have caused this. Because if there is a reason for the spike, then you might be able to stop it. I see you doubting yourself, wondering if you did something "wrong". Ready to blame yourself if you can pin the cause on something you should have done differently.

Please stop. I know how tempting it is to dissect your life, looking for reasons for this spike. But I also know how stressed and anxious it is making you, too.

This spike is not your fault. Tinnitus is not your fault. Just breathe that in. Repeat it over and over until you believe it. You **can** get through this. The spike will quieten down, I promise.

Until then, know that I am with you. I am here for you. Always.

Love,

Jesus

Be strong AND TAKE HEART ALL YOU WHO Hope IN THE LORD

Psalm 31:24 (NIV)

When silence seems a distant memory

Dear beloved tinnitus warrior,

I see you. I know you're worrying whether you're ever going to hear silence again. You will, I can assure you of that. Keep your faith, and when we meet, you will hear blessed silence alongside my voice welcoming you home.

The whistles, pings, trains, planes, clicking and ticking will be gone, replaced with the sound of angels, and loved ones thrilled to see you again.

And until then, I hear you ask? Until then, I am with you every step of the way through these challenging times. I walked on this earth. I hurt, I got sick, and I struggled like you. I know your pain.

Lean on me. Talk to me. Groan and complain at me. And never forget that I am a mere breath away whenever you need me.

Love,

Jesus

BE JOYFUL IN *hope*, PATIENT IN *affliction*, FAITHFUL IN *prayer*

Romans 12:12 (NIV)

When you long for the past

Dear beloved tinnitus warrior,

I see you. I see you living in happier memories before tinnitus came.

I understand how tempting it is to stay in the past. It's safe. All the present moment seems to offer is unbearable noise, suffering and frustration. While the future, if you can even bear to think of it, holds worries about a life stripped of silence.

You recall life before tinnitus as being a golden era. And yet our memory can be a slippery trickster. I have known you since you were knitted together in your mother's womb. I have watched your years pass, each containing the highs and lows of happiness and sadness. Your future will be no different.

I came to earth that you might have an abundant life. And I stand by that promise. Your life can be rich and nourishing, exciting and delightful. Yes, even with tinnitus.

You don't need to worry about how that's going to happen in the future. Just hold my hand and take life day by day. Together we will watch the wonder of your life unfurl.

Love,

Jesus

O Lord,
YOU ALONE ARE
MY HOPE
I'VE TRUSTED YOU,
O Lord,
FROM CHILDHOOD
Psalm 71:5 (NLT)

When you struggle at work

Dear beloved tinnitus warrior,

I see you. I see you with your head in your hands in despair as you struggle to concentrate at work.

I know how tinnitus is affecting your focus. I've watched you trying to hide this from your colleagues and your boss. And I see how stressed and worried you are, wondering if you might lose your job.

Can you trust me? Really trust me? Scary as it sounds, I want you to explain your situation to your manager. I know it will take great courage on your part. But you're not going to be alone for this.

I'm going to walk in step with you as you do this hard thing. When you need support as you ask for a meeting, I'll be beside you. When you rehearse what you're going to say, I will be listening. When you're explaining about the help you need and how your manager can provide it, I will be sitting in the room next to you, offering you moral support and cheering you on.

Beloved child, you deserve all the support and compassion you're going to ask for. We can do this. Together.

Love,

Jesus

WE HAVE THIS Hope AS AN Anchor FOR THE Soul

FIRM AND SECURE

—— Hebrews 6:19 (NIV) ——

When you need some motivation

Dear beloved tinnitus warrior,

I see you. I see how much you are struggling with your tinnitus today.

Would you do something just for me? Would you think of someone who is also struggling with life and get in touch? It can simply be a text, a message, a postcard... Send them love from both of us.

You could even drop by with something they'd appreciate, like food or flowers or the wonderful creation that is YOU!

Why? Because I need your help. Because you are my hands and feet on this beautiful planet we call home. **You** are my love made real.

And because I know that helping another person will also help you too. When you focus on someone else and their struggles, you become much less aware of your own suffering. I know what a wonderful relief that will be for you.

Love,

Jesus

Therefore,

SINCE WE HAVE

SUCH A

Hope

We Are Very

BOLD

— 2 Corinthians 3:12 (NIV) —

When you hide your struggle from your children

Hello mama, hello dad...

I see you. I see how you wear a mask, so the children don't see how much you're struggling.

You can let your mask slip with me. I already know how much you're hurting. I know it's more than you might be prepared to admit to yourself. So, let's spend time together, just you and me, and you can tell me everything. I don't want to add to your burdens, so we can chat as you commute to work, or walk the dog, or vacuum the house, or clean the car. You don't have to stand on ceremony with me.

Let's talk about everything – it all counts, and it's all interconnected with your tinnitus. If you're up at night because your little one is teething, that affects your tinnitus. If you dream of giving your children the best life but, in reality, you're struggling more than ever to make ends meet, that affects your tinnitus too.

Don't try and get through these challenges alone. I'm here for you at every stage of your life, and theirs.

Love,

Jesus

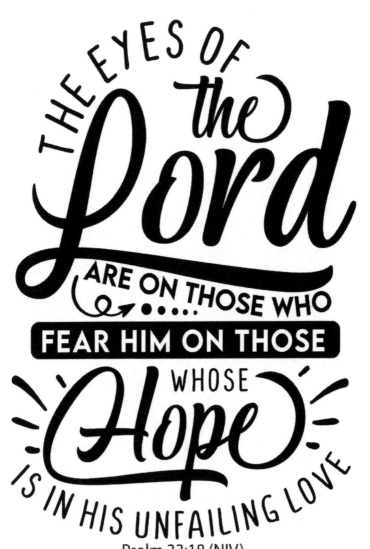

THE EYES OF
the
Lord
ARE ON THOSE WHO
FEAR HIM ON THOSE
WHOSE
Hope
IS IN HIS UNFAILING LOVE
Psalm 33:18 (NIV)

When your family is unsupportive

Dear beloved tinnitus warrior,

I see you. I see how upset and disappointed you are with your family. Your heart is breaking because they just don't understand how hard it can be to live with tinnitus.

Maybe you don't blame them. After all, as the saying goes: you don't **get** tinnitus until you get it. But it still breaks your heart that the people you love don't offer kindness and support when they see how much distress you're in.

I want you to remember there is someone who loves you deeply and understands exactly what you are going through.

Me.

I will always be here for you, ready to listen whenever you want to talk. Just reach out whenever you need me. You can rely on me to give you all the love and support you need.

Love,

Jesus

When
DOUBTS
FILLED MY MIND
your comfort
GAVE ME RENEWED
Hope
AND CHEER

Psalm 94:19 (NLT)

When you struggle in a noisy place

Dear beloved tinnitus warrior,

I see you. I see you sitting in this noisy place and wondering how much longer you can cope. I know you want to be here – whether it's to watch your kids in a sports game or meet friends in a restaurant. But I can also see how much you wish you could be somewhere quieter; a place where your tinnitus doesn't try and compete with all the other noise.

You're trying to grin and bear it, but all the while you're worried about the impact this noise will have on your tinnitus. Will it get louder? If it does, how long will it stay like that? Will you regret coming here tomorrow?

It breaks my heart to see how the joy-full life I hoped for you is overshadowed by this noise. You, who I have known and loved since before you were born.

And I want to tell you that life will not always be like this. That it will get better. That you will be able to go to noisy places and enjoy the reason that you're there.

(continued over the page)

✝ O Israel, ✝

HOPE

in the Lord;

FOR WITH THE

LORD

there is unfailing love.

Psalm 130:7 (NLT)

And if your tinnitus does increase a little as a result of being there, you'll reach the point of being able to shrug it off, knowing it's only a temporary change.

Until then I want you to imagine that I am there – in that gym or stadium or restaurant, bar or cafe – sitting nearby. And when it all becomes a bit too much you can look across at me, and I will smile with eyes of understanding and compassion. And you will know with absolute certainty that you can cope. For you are loved beyond measure.

Love,

Jesus

JOYFUL ARE THOSE WHO HAVE THE GOD OF ISRAEL AS THEIR HELPER, WHOSE HOPE is in the Lord THEIR GOD.

— Psalm 146:5 (NLT) —

When you feel betrayed by your friends

Dear beloved tinnitus warrior,

I see you. I see how hurt you are about those friends who have disappeared from your life. How betrayed you feel when you realise that they have stopped inviting you out because of your struggle with tinnitus.

The people who you thought you could depend on 100% have slowly faded from your life, just when you need their compassion and encouragement the most.

I've known betrayal too. I have been crushed by the rejection of those I thought loved me most. I knew it would come, because this is not Eden, and humans aren't perfect.

So I am sending you new friends; new companions on your tinnitus journey. People who will empathise and lift you up. They might appear in unexpected places so keep a look out!

And I will always be here. Your friend and counsellor. Your guide through this hard time of disappointment and distress. You can always count on me.

Love,

Jesus

Those Who **Hope** IN THE LORD Will Renew Their *Strength.* They will soar on **WINGS** *like Eagles*

Isaiah 40:31 (NIV)

When you feel tinnitus has won

Dear beloved tinnitus warrior,

I see you. I see how much you are struggling with your tinnitus today.

I see how beaten down you feel, how the weight of your life with tinnitus is crushing you; crushing your soul and your spirit.

Keep looking up. Keep looking ahead. Better times will come, I promise you that. Just keep breathing. Just keep moving forward one difficult step after another.

Don't forget I am here for you every. single. second. You might think you can't feel me, but I am there, arms stretched out, ready to lift you up, ready to pull you into my embrace.

Sink into my arms and let me hold you. This is not a time-limited hug. We can stay like this as long as you need to; until you feel ready to take the next step.

Love,

Jesus

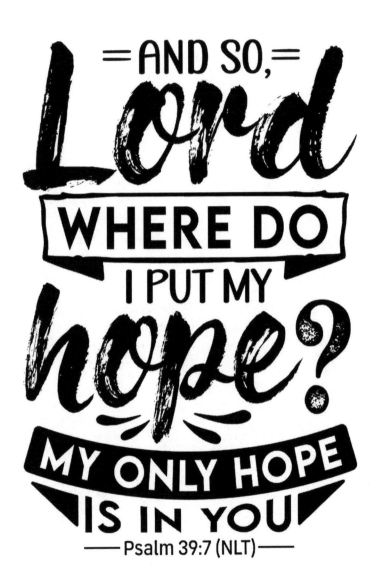

AND SO, Lord WHERE DO I PUT MY hope? MY ONLY HOPE IS IN YOU

Psalm 39:7 (NLT)

When you feel you can't go on

(Content warning: suicide)

Dear beloved tinnitus warrior,

I see you. I see you wondering whether you have the strength to go on. Whether the life you have is worth the effort. Whether it would be easier to call it quits.

I feel your distress, your agony deep in my bones and it makes me want to howl that you – one of God's beloved children – are in so much despair.

I'm here, right beside you, in all your pain and suffering. Can you sense me? Can you feel me wrapping my arms around you as your tears fall, as you are numb, as you think you're beyond any help?

I want you to understand without a shadow of a doubt that your life here has not finished. When the time comes I will be waiting for you BUT this is not your time. This is not your ending.

Beautiful creation of God, you are so precious to me. I love you beyond measure.

(continued over the page)

THE LORD

IS GOOD TO THOSE

WHOSE

Hope

...IS IN HIM,

to the one who

SEEKS HIM

Lamentations 3:25 (NIV)

Lean into me during this horrible time. Let me hold you until your tears run dry. Let me hold you as you stare vacantly into a future you're not sure you want to experience.

Let me hold you until you realise that you have so much more to **give** and **be** and **do** in the world. That your place is here.

And remember, I will be with you – always.

Love,

Jesus

Note from Lisa

If you feel you can't go on, please also reach out for help – to friends, family, or health care professionals. A great place to look for supportive organisations in your country is https://www.psychologytoday.com/us/basics/suicide/suicide-prevention-hotlines-resources-worldwide

AS FOR ME, I WILL

ALWAYS HAVE

Hope;

I WILL

PRAISE

you more

AND MORE

Psalm 71:14 (NIV)

When you feel abandoned by God

Dear beloved tinnitus warrior,

I see you. I see how abandoned you feel. It seems like you are travelling this tinnitus journey alone. You're wondering whether heaven can hear your prayers, your hurt, your desperation, and distress.

We can. I can. I hear every groan that you make. I see every tear fall.

I love you and would **never** abandon you. I am walking alongside you on **all** your life journeys.

Don't believe me? Close your eyes right now and hold out your hand. Can you see me place my hand in yours? Do you feel the warmth of our contact, the firm grip I have? Have faith that I am holding you tight. I will never let you fall.

I have the map, and I know the destination. So, keep your eyes on me and place your feet in my footprints. Together we will travel through the hills and valleys of tinnitus, hand-in-hand and heart-with-heart.

Love,

Jesus

MAY THE
God
of hope
FILL YOU WITH ALL
JOY & PEACE
as you
Trust in Him
Romans 15:13 (NIV)

When you start to accept your tinnitus

Dear tinnitus warrior,

So, you think you've cracked this thing called tinnitus? Sure, the noises are there, but they don't bother you as much as they used to. I am SO delighted!

You might not have noticed me, but I've been walking beside you, cheering you on. And I have to tell you I've watched you grow beautifully through such a challenging time. I am **so** proud of you.

You have gained resilience and tinnitus wisdom that is incredibly valuable to another warrior just starting out on their journey. Will you extend a hand of hope to them?

You are the best proof that life with tinnitus can still be joy-full. And someone out there needs to hear that so very much. Would you be my voice of reassurance?

Please reach out to a fellow warrior today for me. Let them know that however bad they feel things are, they will get better. **You** are the living, breathing, loving proof of that.

Love,

Jesus

Thank you!

My heartfelt thanks go to:

- Sean, my husband, for your love and support

- Ziva, our Romanian rescue dog, for dragging me away from the desk to get some fresh air

- My lovely friends at the London Writers Salon (www.londonwriterssalon.com) who have written alongside me since 2020, especially Jenny Hammerton (www.silverscreensuppers.com) and Sam Kilgour (www.samkilgour.com), my accountability buddies, and everyone in the Gold group and Cabin who have cheered me on

- Author Joy Vee (www.joyvee.org) for her wonderful proof-reading skills

- All the beloved tinnitus warriors I have had the privilege of meeting and coaching over the years

- God, of course, for picking me up and dusting me down more times than I can count, and for giving me the gift of words

About Lisa

Lisa has lived with tinnitus since 2005 when she suddenly lost her hearing in one ear and gained tinnitus in its place. Her hearing has never returned, and the tinnitus has never left.

The tinnitus she experiences is a combination of airplane engines and electrical pylons together with random beeps as and when they feel like joining in! It can be loud enough to block out the sound of the TV and conversation. But in spite of all that noise, Lisa's tinnitus no longer bothers her.

She uses her lived experience of overcoming her struggles with tinnitus to coach others around the world who feel as lost, frustrated, anxious and depressed as she did early in her tinnitus journey.

Lisa lives in England with her husband and her rescue dog. When not working she can be found with her family in their little caravan exploring the UK and Europe.

To find out more about Lisa and the faith-based hope she offers, visit www.faithhopetinnitus.com

Printed in Great Britain
by Amazon

28807487R00026